THIS IS MAURO

ASSAGGIO RISTORANTE COOKBOOK

HAPPY 50 th
You Are Getting
Better when so
with This Book
I AM with You
when You Are cook

MAURO GOLMARVI

THIS IS MAURO

ASSAGGIO RISTORANTE COOKBOOK

PHOTOGRAPHY BY JONATHAN BARTA

DOCUMENTARY MEDIA, SEATTLE

First edition 2013
Printed in Canada

ISBN 978-1-933245-29-4

by Mauro Golmarvi
Recipes developed by Mauro Golmarvi
Food photography by Jonathan Barta
Food Styling by Jonathan Barta and
    Michel McCammon
Designed by Michel McCammon
Edited by Judy Gouldthorpe

Published by Documentary Media
3250 41st Avenue SW
Seattle, WA 98116
www.documentarymedia.com
books@docbooks.com

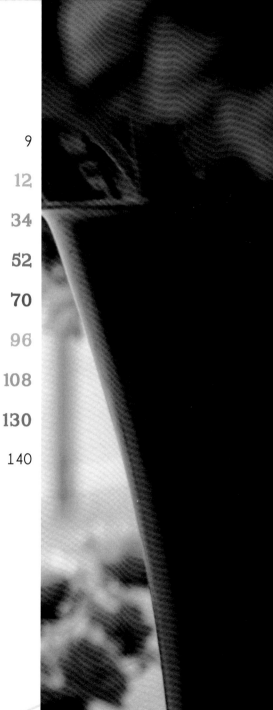

CONTENTS

HELLO, GORGEOUS!

I HAD THE IDEA FOR MY SECOND COOKBOOK FOR A
LONG TIME. THERE WERE LOTS OF THINGS I WANTED TO
SHARE IN MY FIRST BOOK BUT COULDN'T BECAUSE NOT
ENOUGH PAGES. NOW THROUGH YOUR SUPPORT, I AM ABLE
TO SHARE MORE OF WHAT I LOVE, MORE OF MY PASSION.

I DECIDED TO DO SAME THING, SAME IDEA: SIMPLE.
BOTH BOOKS FOCUS ON SIMPLE. USE FRESH INGREDIENTS
TO MAKE SIMPLE, PASSION-FILLED ITEMS. NO COMPLICATIONS.
WHEN PEOPLE SAY FUSION, I CALL IT CONFUSION. I ALWAYS
ASK WAITERS WHO BRING ME PERFECTLY STACKED FOOD,
"DO YOU EAT LIKE THIS AT HOME? NO, OF COURSE NOT!"

YOU WILL FIND ONLY SIMPLE, FLAVORFUL RECIPES HERE.
MY CACIO E PEPE RECIPE IS SPAGHETTI, BLACK PEPPER,
CHEESE AND OLIVE OIL. THE INGREDIENTS MAKE IT A
POWERFUL DISH AND PERFECT FOR ANY FAMILY MEAL.
I WANT YOU TO CONNECT WITH THE EARTH AND USE THIS
TO FOCUS ON THE INGREDIENTS. FROM FRESH FISH WITH
SIMPLE SAUCES TO ANY TABLE WINE. THE MORE SIMPLE,
THE MORE FLAVOR.

THIS YEAR IS ASSAGGIO'S 20TH ANNIVERSARY, AND THIS COOKBOOK IS NOT ABOUT MAKING MONEY. IT'S NOT ABOUT BEING FAMOUS. IT'S ABOUT ME HAVING A PIECE OF EVERYBODY'S HOME. I WANT TO BE A PART OF YOUR FAMILY AS I MAKE YOU A PART OF MINE. MY RESTAURANT IS YOUR HOME. YOUR TABLE IS IN MY LIVING ROOM, AND I WANT YOU TO REMEMBER THE FEELING YOU HAVE WHEN EATING MY FOOD LONG AFTER YOU LEAVE MY RESTAURANT. THIS BOOK IS FOR EVERYBODY. IT'S FOR WHEN MY DAUGHTER, FRANCESCA, WALKS DOWN THE AISLE AND HAS KIDS. SHE CAN ALWAYS OPEN THIS BOOK AND MAKE HER FAVORITE, PANZANELLA SALAD, FOR HER FAMILY. SHE LIKES TO EAT SIMPLE; GREW UP ON SIMPLICITY. THIS IS MY LEGACY FOR HER. SHE ALWAYS SAYS, "DAD CAN MAKE FOOD FROM NOTHING. OPEN ANY CUPBOARD. IF YOU HAVE PASTA AND A CAN OF TOMATOES, HE CAN MAKE A BIG, CELEBRATION MEAL FOR EVERYONE."

LET'S CELEBRATE TOGETHER AND START COOKING!

ANTIPASTO

POMODORI RIPIENI
STUFFED TOMATOES **15**

MOZZARELLA IN CARROZZA
MOZZARELLA WITH BREAD **16**

PETTINI DI MARE SCOTTATI
SEARED SCALLOPS **18**

LATTUGA STUFATA
BRAISED LETTUCE **19**

SCAMPI E GAMBERETTI
SHRIMP SCAMPI **21**

CALAMARI FRITTI
FRIED CALAMARI **23**

GNOCCO FRITTO
FRIED BREAD WITH PROSCIUTTO **27**

VONGOLE RIPIENE
STUFFED CLAMS **28**

FRITTO MISTO DI VEGETALI
FRIED VEGETABLES WITH MUSTARD DIP **30**

SPINACI
SAUTÉED SPINACH **31**

OLIVE CON NOCI
OLIVE SPREAD WITH WALNUTS **33**

YOU ARE IN MIDDLE OF SUMMER AND HAVE BEAUTIFUL, FRESH TOMATOES. AT SOME POINT, TOO MANY, WHICH MEANS FALL IS COMING. AS A SALUTE TO FALL, YOU MUST MAKE STUFFED TOMATOES AND FORGET THE COLD OF SALADS.

POMODORI RIPIENI
STUFFED TOMATOES
SERVES 2

INGREDIENTS

2 LARGE HEIRLOOM TOMATOES

1 CUP SPINACH

1/2 CUP RICOTTA CHEESE

2 TEASPOONS CHOPPED FRESH
    PARSLEY

2 TEASPOONS FRESH OREGANO

2 EGGS

SALT AND PEPPER

INSTRUCTIONS

Preheat oven to 425°F.

Cut a hole around the tomato stem and scoop out the middle with a spoon. Turn the tomato over and drain excess liquid. Season with salt. Repeat. Place the tomatoes on a foil-lined baking sheet and cook in the oven for 5 minutes. Remove from the oven and flip the tomatoes to drain.

In a large sauté pan over medium-high heat, cook spinach until it wilts. In a small bowl, combine spinach, ricotta, parsley, oregano, salt and pepper.

Scoop the mixture into the tomatoes, leaving room for the egg at the top. Crack one egg into each tomato, letting it rest on top of the cheese mixture.

Place the sheet in the oven and bake for 8 minutes, or until the eggs are cooked to taste. Remove from the oven and serve.

THIS SICILIAN PEASANT DISH IS FOR WHEN SUMMER IS OVER AND YOU HAVE OLD BREAD AND MOZZARELLA. YOU DON'T KNOW WHAT TO DO WITH THEM. SO YOU COMBINE EGG AND FLOUR. FRY IT AND DONE.

MOZZARELLA IN CARROZZA
MOZZARELLA WITH BREAD
SERVES 2

INGREDIENTS

5 OUNCES FRESH MOZZARELLA,
   CUT INTO STRIPS
4 SLICES SOURDOUGH BREAD
1/2 CUP WHOLE MILK
3 TABLESPOONS ALL-PURPOSE
   FLOUR
1 EGG
1/2 CUP EXTRA-VIRGIN OLIVE OIL
SALT AND PEPPER

INSTRUCTIONS

Place half of the mozzarella between 2 slices of bread and firmly press down. Repeat the step.

Pour milk and flour into separate medium bowls. Whisk egg in another medium bowl and add salt and pepper.

In a large skillet, heat olive oil over medium heat until shimmering. Dredge each side of the sandwiches in the milk, then the flour and lastly, the beaten egg. Fry each side of the sandwiches in oil until golden brown. Cut in half and serve.

PETTINI DI MARE SCOTTATI
SEARED SCALLOPS
SERVES 4

INGREDIENTS

1 POUND SEA SCALLOPS
2 TEASPOONS UNSALTED BUTTER
2 TEASPOONS EXTRA-VIRGIN
  OLIVE OIL
SALT AND PEPPER

INSTRUCTIONS

Rinse scallops with cold water and pat dry with a paper towel. Season with salt and pepper.

In a large sauté pan over medium-high heat, add butter and olive oil. Once the pan starts to smoke, add the scallops, making sure they aren't touching. Sear the scallops for 1 to 2 minutes on each side. Each scallop should have a golden crust ring, while being translucent in the center. Serve.

YOU HAVE TO REMEMBER THERE ARE ALL KINDS OF WAYS TO HAVE LETTUCE. NOT JUST SALAD, SALAD, SALAD. WHEN IT'S WINTER YOU MUST BRAISE LETTUCE TO BRING WARMTH TO YOUR KITCHEN AND HOME.

LATTUGA STUFATA
BRAISED LETTUCE
SERVES 4

INGREDIENTS

6 HEADS BIBB LETTUCE, TRIMMED, RINSED

2 TABLESPOONS EXTRA-VIRGIN OLIVE OIL

1/4 CUP DICED RED ONION

1/2 CUP DICED CELERY

2 CUPS VEGETABLE BROTH (PAGE 68)

1/2 TEASPOON DRIED THYME

SALT AND PEPPER

INSTRUCTIONS

In a large pot, bring 6 quarts of salted water to a boil. Blanch lettuce for 3 minutes. Drain and squeeze dry. Season with salt and pepper.

In a large skillet, heat olive oil over medium heat until shimmering. Add red onion and celery. Cook until soft.

Place the lettuce heads in the skillet and spoon onion and celery over the top. Add vegetable broth, covering the lettuce. Add thyme. Bring the broth to a boil over high heat.

Cover the skillet and reduce the heat to low, simmering until tender, about 25 minutes. Serve.

SCAMPI E GAMBERETTI

SHRIMP SCAMPI

SERVES 4

INGREDIENTS

2 TABLESPOONS UNSALTED
  BUTTER
1 1/2 POUNDS JUMBO SHRIMP,
  SHELLED, DEVEINED
2 TEASPOONS MINCED GARLIC
1/4 CUP DRY WHITE WINE
1 TABLESPOON LEMON JUICE
2 TEASPOONS CHOPPED FRESH
  PARSLEY
SALT AND PEPPER

INSTRUCTIONS

In a large skillet, melt butter over medium heat. Season shrimp with salt and pepper.

Increase the skillet heat to high. Add the shrimp and cook for 1 minute without moving them. Add garlic and cook for 1 minute. Turn the shrimp over and cook for 2 minutes. Remove from the skillet.

Pour wine and lemon juice into the heated skillet. Bring to a boil and cook for 30 seconds. Stir in parsley. Pour the sauce over the shrimp and serve.

EVERYBODY LOVES SEAFOOD, AND ONCE IN A WHILE YOU WANT THAT SATURATED OIL IN YOUR BODY. NOT ALWAYS EATING HEALTHY IS OKAY. ADDS SPICE.

CALAMARI FRITTI
FRIED CALAMARI
SERVES 4

INGREDIENTS

VEGETABLE OIL, FOR FRYING

2 CUPS ALL-PURPOSE FLOUR

1 TEASPOON DRIED OREGANO

1 TEASPOON KOSHER SALT

1/2 TEASPOON GROUND
   BLACK PEPPER

1 POUND SQUID WITH TENTACLES,
   CLEANED, BODIES CUT INTO
   1/2-INCH RINGS

2 TEASPOONS CHOPPED FRESH
   PARSLEY

1 CUP MARINARA (PAGE 94)

2 LEMONS, CUT INTO WEDGES

INSTRUCTIONS

Fill a large pot 1/3 full of vegetable oil and heat over medium-high heat to 350°F.

In a large bowl, mix flour, oregano, salt and pepper. Toss small batches of squid into the flour mixture, coating the squid. Slowly add the squid to the hot oil and fry for 1 minute, or until golden brown.

Using a slotted spoon, transfer the squid to a plate lined with a paper towel. Garnish with the parsley. Serve with marinara and lemons.

GNOCCO FRITTO
FRIED BREAD WITH PROSCIUTTO
SERVES 6

INGREDIENTS

2/3 CUP WHOLE MILK

1 PACKAGE ACTIVE DRY YEAST

3 CUPS ALL-PURPOSE FLOUR

1 TABLESPOON EXTRA-VIRGIN
  OLIVE OIL

1 TEASPOON SALT

VEGETABLE OIL, FOR FRYING

1 POUND PROSCIUTTO, THINLY
  SLICED (OR OTHER DELI MEATS)

INSTRUCTIONS

In a small saucepan, bring milk to a simmer over medium-low heat. Remove from the heat and dissolve yeast into the milk.

In a large bowl, combine the yeast mixture, flour, olive oil and salt. Cover the dough with a damp cloth and let rise for 1 hour in a warm, dry area.

Fill a large pot 1/3 full of vegetable oil and heat over medium-high heat to 350°F.

Cut the dough into egg-sized pieces and cook in small batches in the hot oil until golden brown. Remove and dry on paper towels.

Place a slice of prosciutto on each piece and serve.

WHEN YOU HAVE CLAMS, FIRST DAY IS PERFECT. SECOND DAY YOU MUST COOK, AND THIRD DAY YOU THROW OUT. STUFFING AND BAKING CLAMS GIVES DIFFERENT ELEMENT FROM FIRST DAY, DIFFERENT FEEL. PERFECT FOR SMALL BITE.

VONGOLE RIPIENE
STUFFED CLAMS
SERVES 4

INGREDIENTS

3 TABLESPOONS EXTRA-VIRGIN
   OLIVE OIL
4 OUNCES PANCETTA, DICED
1/4 SMALL WHITE ONION, CHOPPED
1/4 CUP CHOPPED FRESH PARSLEY
1/2 CUP PLUS 1/4 CUP FRESH
   BREAD CRUMBS
12 CLAMS, SHUCKED AND
   JUICE RESERVED, SHELLS SAVED
1 LEMON, JUICED
DRY WHITE WINE
SALT AND PEPPER

INSTRUCTIONS

Preheat oven to broil.

In a large skillet, heat 1 tablespoon olive oil over medium heat until shimmering. Add pancetta and cook until the fat is rendered.

With a slotted spoon, transfer the pancetta to a medium bowl. Add onion, parsley and 1/2 cup bread crumbs. Dice clams into small chunks and add to the mixture. Add reserved clam juice. Season with salt, pepper and lemon juice. Fill the clam shells with the mixture and place on a baking sheet.

In a large skillet, heat remaining olive oil over medium heat and add a splash of white wine to taste. Drizzle each clam with the sauce and top with remaining bread crumbs. Broil until browned. Serve.

rosemary

THIS RECIPE IS THE ITALIAN VERSION OF TEMPURA. IT IS GOOD AND HEARTY. PERFECT FOR SMALL BITE.

FRITTO MISTO DI VEGETALI
FRIED VEGETABLES WITH MUSTARD DIP
SERVES 4

INGREDIENTS

VEGETABLE OIL, FOR FRYING
1 1/2 CUPS ALL-PURPOSE FLOUR
1 SMALL CAULIFLOWER, CUT INTO
   1-INCH PIECES
1 CUP CANNED CANNELLINI BEANS
1 FENNEL BULB, MIDDLE REMOVED,
   SLICED INTO 1-INCH PIECES
1 ZUCCHINI, CUT INTO
   1-INCH PIECES
1 LEMON, CUT INTO WEDGES
SALT AND PEPPER
KOSHER SALT

DIP
1 CUP STONE-GROUND MUSTARD
2 TABLESPOONS LEMON JUICE
1 TEASPOON MINCED GARLIC

INSTRUCTIONS

Fill a large pot 1/3 full of vegetable oil and heat over medium-high heat to 350°F.

In a medium bowl, combine flour and salt and pepper to taste. Dredge cauliflower, beans, fennel, zucchini and lemon in the flour. Fry the ingredients until golden brown.

Drain on a paper towel and sprinkle with kosher salt. Serve with dip.

DIP
In a small bowl, whisk mustard, lemon juice and garlic together until smooth.

THIS IS MAURO

30

SPINACI
SAUTÉED SPINACH
SERVES 4

INGREDIENTS

10 CUPS SPINACH
1/4 CUP EXTRA-VIRGIN OLIVE OIL
2 TABLESPOONS MINCED GARLIC
1/4 CUP PINE NUTS, TOASTED
1 LEMON, JUICED
SALT

INSTRUCTIONS

In a large pot, bring 6 quarts of salted water to a boil. Add spinach and blanch for 30 seconds. Remove and place in ice water. Immediately remove once cooled and squeeze out excess water.

In a large sauté pan, heat olive oil over medium heat until shimmering. Add garlic and cook for 1 minute, or until golden brown. Add the spinach, pine nuts, lemon juice and salt. Sauté for 2 minutes. Serve.

OLIVE SPREAD IS ONE OF MY MOM'S FAVORITE FOODS. I GREW UP KNOWING IT WAS ALWAYS AVAILABLE. HERE IS A MODIFIED VERSION.

OLIVE CON NOCI
OLIVE SPREAD WITH WALNUTS
SERVES 4

INGREDIENTS

1 1/2 CUPS PITTED KALAMATA
  OLIVES
3/4 CUP WALNUTS, TOASTED
  AND CHOPPED
1/4 CUP EXTRA-VIRGIN OLIVE OIL
2 TEASPOONS STONE-GROUND
  MUSTARD
2 CLOVES GARLIC, MINCED
1 TEASPOON FRESH THYME
1 TEASPOON FRESH OREGANO
1 TEASPOON FRESH SAGE
1/2 CUP DRIED OR FRESH
  CRANBERRIES

INSTRUCTIONS

In a food processor, finely chop olives and 3 tablespoons of walnuts. Add olive oil, mustard, garlic, thyme, oregano, sage and cranberries. Process until coarsely puréed.

Stir in remaining walnuts. Serve with bread.

INSALATA

INSALATA DI POLIPO
OCTOPUS SALAD **36**

INSALATA DI PANZANELLA
BREAD SALAD **38**

CHOP-CHOP-CHEF
ITALIAN CHOPPED SALAD **41**

INSALATA DI FRANCESCA
APPLE, PEAR AND PISTACHIO SALAD **43**

INSALATA DI PERA CON RUCOLA
ARUGULA AND PEAR SALAD **47**

BRASATO DI BIETOLA
BRAISED CHARD **48**

INSALATA DI FARRO E POMODORI
FARRO WITH TOMATOES **49**

INSALATA DI ARANCE E FINOCCHI
ORANGE FENNEL SALAD **50**

IN ITALY, DURING THE HOT SUMMER AFTERNOON, YOU DON'T KNOW WHAT YOU ARE GOING TO EAT. YOU'RE DONE WITH THE MIDDAY PROSCIUTTO AND HAVE CHILLED OCTOPUS FROM NIGHT BEFORE. THESE INGREDIENTS WORK PERFECT WHEN YOU DON'T KNOW.

INSALATA DI POLIPO
OCTOPUS SALAD
SERVES 4

INGREDIENTS

1 OCTOPUS (4 POUNDS)
4 CELERY STALKS, DICED
4 LEMONS, JUICED
1 CUP PITTED KALAMATA OLIVES, DICED
3 CLOVES GARLIC, MINCED
1/4 SMALL RED ONION, DICED
8 STEMS ITALIAN PARSLEY, DICED
6 BASIL LEAVES, CHOPPED
EXTRA-VIRGIN OLIVE OIL
SALT AND PEPPER

INSTRUCTIONS

Place octopus in a large pot and fill with water until the octopus is submerged. Bring to a boil and cook on medium-low heat, uncovered, until tender, about 2 hours.

Remove the octopus from the water and let cool. Slice into small pieces.

In a large bowl, combine octopus, celery, lemon juice, olives, garlic, onion, parsley and basil. Sprinkle with olive oil. Mix well, seasoning with salt and pepper to taste.

Serve at room temperature.

THIS IS MAURO

THIS IS FRANCESCA'S RECIPE. OUR CREATION TOGETHER. IT IS HER ABSOLUTE FAVORITE AND WE EAT IT ALL THE TIME DURING THE SUMMER MONTHS.

INSALATA DI PANZANELLA
BREAD SALAD
SERVES 4

INGREDIENTS

1/2 POUND DARK BREAD,
   GRILLED OR TOASTED, CUT INTO
   3/4-INCH CUBES
6 TOMATOES, DICED
1 POUND FRESH MOZZARELLA,
   CUT INTO 3/4-INCH CUBES
1/2 CUP DICED RED ONION
1/3 CUP CHOPPED FRESH BASIL
1 TABLESPOON CHOPPED FRESH
   ITALIAN PARSLEY
1/4 CUP EXTRA-VIRGIN OLIVE OIL
3 TABLESPOONS COLD WATER
SALT AND PEPPER

INSTRUCTIONS

In a large bowl, combine bread, tomatoes, mozzarella, onion, basil and parsley. Stir in olive oil, water, salt and pepper.

Mix the ingredients well with your hands. Let stand for 20 minutes.

Serve.

CHOP-CHOP-CHEF
ITALIAN CHOPPED SALAD
SERVES 4

INGREDIENTS

2 CUPS CHOPPED ROMAINE
  LETTUCE
2 CUPS CHOPPED ARUGULA
2 CUPS CHOPPED RADICCHIO
2 CUPS CHOPPED SPINACH
1 CUP CANNED CANNELLINI BEANS
10 OIL-PACKED SUN-DRIED TOMATO
  HALVES, DRAINED, CUT INTO
  THIN SLICES

DRESSING

2 TABLESPOONS RED WINE
  VINEGAR
6 TABLESPOONS EXTRA-VIRGIN
  OLIVE OIL
SALT AND PEPPER

INSTRUCTIONS

In a large bowl, combine lettuce, arugula, radicchio, spinach, beans and sun-dried tomatoes. Drizzle the desired amount of dressing over the lettuce mixture. Toss to coat. Serve.

DRESSING
In a bowl, whisk vinegar with salt and pepper to taste. Slowly whisk in olive oil until blended.

INSALATA DI FRANCESCA
APPLE, PEAR AND PISTACHIO SALAD
SERVES 4

INGREDIENTS

1 GREEN APPLE, CORED, SLICED
1 PEAR, CORED, SLICED
1/2 CUP CRUMBLED GORGONZOLA
1/2 CUP CANDIED PISTACHIOS
4 CUPS ITALIAN MIXED GREENS

Vinaigrette

1 TEASPOON DIJON MUSTARD
3 TABLESPOONS RED WINE
   VINEGAR
1 TEASPOON DRIED OREGANO
1 TEASPOON DRIED ROSEMARY
1 CLOVE GARLIC, MINCED
1/2 TEASPOON SALT
1/2 TEASPOON GROUND BLACK
   PEPPER
1/2 CUP EXTRA-VIRGIN OLIVE OIL

Candied Pistachios

3 CUPS WATER
1 CUP RAW SHELLED PISTACHIOS
1/3 CUP CONFECTIONERS' SUGAR
3 TABLESPOONS VEGETABLE OIL

INSTRUCTIONS

In a large bowl, combine apple, pear, Gorgonzola, pistachios and greens. Toss with vinaigrette to coat.

VINAIGRETTE

In a large bowl, whisk together mustard, vinegar, oregano, rosemary, garlic, salt and pepper. Slowly whisk in olive oil until combined.

CANDIED PISTACHIOS

In a medium saucepan, bring water to a boil over medium heat. Add pistachios to the boiling water and blanch for 1 minute. Drain into a colander and rinse with cold water. Transfer the pistachios to a medium bowl and add sugar, stirring to combine well.

In a medium sauté pan, heat oil over medium-high heat. When the oil starts to smoke, pour in the pistachio mixture and cook until the pistachios are golden brown, stirring often. Pour the mixture into a colander and shake out onto a plate. Break apart any pieces that are stuck together.

IN ITALIAN, ARUGULA MEANS ROCKET. IT'S WILD AND GROWS EVERYWHERE. IN WASHINGTON, THE PEAR IS A STAPLE FOR US. I CREATED THIS RECIPE TO MARRY WASHINGTON AND ITALY WITH THE SWEETNESS OF THE FRUIT AND THE SOURNESS OF THE ARUGULA.

INSALATA DI PERA CON RUCOLA
ARUGULA AND PEAR SALAD
SERVES 6

INGREDIENTS

6 CUPS ARUGULA

2 PEARS, CORED, SLICED

2/3 CUP WALNUT HALVES,
   TOASTED

1 BLOOD ORANGE, JUICED

4 TABLESPOONS EXTRA-VIRGIN
   OLIVE OIL

8 OUNCES CRUMBLED
   GORGONZOLA

SALT AND PEPPER

INSTRUCTIONS

In a large bowl, combine arugula and pears. Add walnuts.

Dress the salad with orange juice and olive oil. Season with salt and pepper. Top each serving with Gorgonzola crumbles.

BRASATO DI BIETOLA

BRAISED CHARD

SERVES 4

INGREDIENTS

2 BUNCHES SWISS CHARD,
   WASHED, DRIED
3 TABLESPOONS EXTRA-VIRGIN
   OLIVE OIL
1/4 MEDIUM WHITE ONION, DICED
4 ANCHOVY FILLETS, CHOPPED
2 TABLESPOONS GOLDEN RAISINS
2 TEASPOONS CAPERS
2 CLOVES GARLIC, MINCED
1/2 CUP PITTED KALAMATA OLIVES,
   CHOPPED
2 TABLESPOONS PINE NUTS,
   TOASTED
1/2 CUP SUNFLOWER SEEDS
1 TABLESPOON LEMON JUICE
SALT AND PEPPER

INSTRUCTIONS

Remove chard stems and set aside. Cut the chard leaves into 1-inch strips.

In a medium pan, heat olive oil over medium heat until shimmering. Add onion, anchovies and raisins. Cook until the onion is translucent, stirring occasionally. Add capers and garlic, and cook until the garlic is golden brown. Add the chard stems and cook for 2 minutes, or until the stems start to brown. Add the chard leaves and cook for 5 minutes, or until wilted.

Stir in olives, pine nuts, sunflower seeds and lemon juice. Season with salt and pepper. Serve.

INSALATA DI FARRO E POMODORI
FARRO WITH TOMATOES
SERVES 6

INGREDIENTS

3 CUPS WATER

1 1/2 CUPS FARRO

1 POUND HEIRLOOM TOMATOES,
    SEEDED, CHOPPED

1/4 SMALL RED ONION, CHOPPED

1/4 CUP CHOPPED FRESH CHIVES

1/4 CUP CHOPPED FRESH PARSLEY

1 CLOVE GARLIC, MINCED

2 TABLESPOONS BALSAMIC
    VINEGAR

1/4 CUP EXTRA-VIRGIN OLIVE OIL

SALT AND PEPPER

INSTRUCTIONS

In a medium saucepan, combine water and farro. Add salt to taste. Bring to a boil over high heat. Reduce the heat, cover and simmer for 30 minutes, or until the farro is tender. Drain and cool.

In a large bowl, combine farro, tomatoes, onion, chives and parsley.

In a medium bowl, whisk together garlic, vinegar, olive oil, salt and pepper. Add to the salad and toss together. Serve.

THIS IS A TYPICAL SICILIAN DISH. YOU HAVE TO HAVE THE BEST ORANGES POSSIBLE. IT'S COMPLETELY A FALL SALAD BECAUSE THE FENNEL IS UNDERGROUND AND THE ORANGE IS A FALL FRUIT.

INSALATA DI ARANCE E FINOCCHI
ORANGE FENNEL SALAD
SERVES 6

INGREDIENTS

4 BLOOD ORANGES, PEELED, SLICED
1 LARGE FENNEL BULB, MIDDLE
   REMOVED, SLICED
1 POUND ARUGULA

DRESSING
2 LARGE LEMONS, JUICED
1/4 CUP EXTRA-VIRGIN OLIVE OIL
SALT AND PEPPER

INSTRUCTIONS

In a large bowl, combine oranges, fennel and arugula. Toss with dressing and serve.

DRESSING
In a small bowl, combine lemon juice, olive oil, and salt and pepper to taste. Whisk until combined.

ZUPPE

BRODETTO
SEAFOOD SOUP **54**

CIOPPINO
SEAFOOD STEW **57**

MINESTRA DI CREMA DI CAROTE
CARROT CREAM SOUP **58**

MINESTRA DI CAVOLFIORE
CAULIFLOWER SOUP **61**

ZUPPA DI MELANZANE
ROASTED EGGPLANT SOUP **62**

MINESTRA DI PISELLI
GREEN PEA SOUP **63**

ZUPPA DI CINGHIALE
WILD BOAR SOUP **67**

BRODO DI PESCE
FISH BROTH **68**

BRODO DI VEGETALE
VEGETABLE BROTH **68**

BRODO DI POLLO
CHICKEN BROTH **69**

BRODETTO
SEAFOOD SOUP
SERVES 6

INGREDIENTS

2 TABLESPOONS UNSALTED
   BUTTER
1/2 POUND SQUID, CUT INTO RINGS
1 POUND MEDIUM MUSSELS,
   SCRUBBED, RINSED, BEARD
   REMOVED
1/2 CUP CHOPPED GREEN ONIONS
1/2 CUP SAFFRON TEA (PAGE 86)
2 CUPS FISH BROTH (PAGE 68)
1 CUP HEAVY CREAM
1 POUND CLAMS, SCRUBBED,
   RINSED
1/2 POUND BAY SCALLOPS
1/2 POUND COOKED BAY SHRIMP
1/4 CUP CHOPPED FRESH PARSLEY
SALT AND PEPPER

INSTRUCTIONS

In a large saucepan, melt butter over medium heat. Add salt and pepper to taste. Add squid and sauté for 2 minutes. Add mussels and onions, sautéing for 2 minutes. Pour in saffron tea, fish broth and cream. Increase the heat to medium-high and cover, bringing to a boil. Add clams and scallops. Cover and cook for 2 minutes. Stir in shrimp. Cover and cook for 2 minutes, or until all the clams have opened.

Transfer immediately to a large serving bowl. Discard any unopened mussels and clams. Garnish with parsley and serve.

CIOPPINO
SEAFOOD STEW
SERVES 6

INGREDIENTS

1/4 CUP EXTRA-VIRGIN OLIVE OIL
1 LARGE WHITE ONION, CHOPPED
4 CLOVES GARLIC, MINCED
2 1/2 TEASPOONS DRIED THYME
2 TEASPOONS DRIED OREGANO
3/4 TEASPOON CRUSHED RED
   PEPPER FLAKES
1 BAY LEAF
1 CAN (28 OUNCES) SAN MARZANO
   TOMATOES, CRUSHED
1 1/2 CUPS CHARDONNAY
3 CUPS FISH BROTH (PAGE 68)
1 POUND MANILA CLAMS,
   SCRUBBED, RINSED
2 POUNDS COD CUT INTO
   SMALL PIECES
1 1/4 POUNDS LARGE SHRIMP,
   SHELLED, DEVEINED
1/2 CUP CHOPPED FRESH PARSLEY
SALT AND PEPPER

INSTRUCTIONS

In a large pot, heat olive oil over medium heat until shimmering. Add onion and garlic, cooking until the onion is translucent. Stir in thyme, oregano, red pepper flakes and bay leaf. Add tomatoes, wine and fish broth.

Bring to a simmer. Add clams and simmer, covered, for 10 minutes, or until the clams open. Season cod with salt and pepper. Add fish and shrimp to the pot. Simmer, covered, until the shrimp are pink, 3 minutes.

Discard the bay leaf and any unopened clams. Stir in parsley. Remove from the heat and serve.

MINESTRA DI CREMA DI CAROTE
CARROT CREAM SOUP
SERVES 6

INGREDIENTS

3 TABLESPOONS EXTRA-VIRGIN
   OLIVE OIL
1 1/2 POUNDS CARROTS, CHOPPED
2 LARGE WHITE ONIONS, CHOPPED
3 CLOVES GARLIC, CHOPPED
3 TABLESPOONS ALL-PURPOSE
   FLOUR
6 CUPS VEGETABLE BROTH
   (PAGE 68)
1 BAY LEAF
1 CUP HEAVY CREAM
1 LEMON, JUICED
SALT AND PEPPER

INSTRUCTIONS

In a large sauté pan over medium-high heat, heat olive oil until shimmering. Add carrots, onions and garlic. Sauté until the onions are translucent. Add flour and cook for 1 minute, stirring constantly. Add vegetable broth and bay leaf. Bring to a boil. Reduce the heat and cover, simmering for 30 minutes.

Remove the bay leaf and purée the mixture in small batches in a food processor. Add cream, lemon juice, salt and pepper. Reheat and simmer for 5 minutes. Remove from the heat and serve.

MINESTRA DI CAVOLFIORE
CAULIFLOWER SOUP
SERVES 6

INGREDIENTS

4 TABLESPOONS EXTRA-VIRGIN
   OLIVE OIL
1 1/2 POUNDS CAULIFLOWER,
   CHOPPED
1 LARGE WHITE ONION, CHOPPED
1 CARROT, CHOPPED
3 TABLESPOONS ALL-PURPOSE
   FLOUR
4 CUPS VEGETABLE BROTH
   (PAGE 68)
1/2 CUP HEAVY CREAM
SALT AND PEPPER

INSTRUCTIONS

In a large sauté pan over medium-high heat, heat olive oil until shimmering. Add cauliflower, onion, carrot, salt and pepper. Sauté until the onion is translucent. Add flour and cook for 1 minute, stirring constantly. Add vegetable broth and bring to a boil.

Reduce the heat to medium-low and simmer, uncovered, for 10 minutes. Add cream.

Purée the mixture in small batches in a food processor. Reheat in a sauté pan over medium heat if cold. Serve.

ZUPPA DI MELANZANE
ROASTED EGGPLANT SOUP
SERVES 6

INGREDIENTS

2 LARGE EGGPLANTS

6 CLOVES GARLIC, PEELED

2 TEASPOONS EXTRA-VIRGIN
   OLIVE OIL

1/4 CUP DICED RED ONION

6 CUPS VEGETABLE BROTH
   (PAGE 68)

1 CUP TOMATO PURÉE

1 PINCH CRUSHED RED PEPPER
   FLAKES

1 CUP HEAVY CREAM

SALT AND PEPPER

INSTRUCTIONS

Preheat oven to 400°F and line a baking sheet with foil. Cut eggplants in half lengthwise. Place skin side down on the baking sheet and bake for 10 minutes.

Rub garlic with 1 teaspoon olive oil and place on the baking sheet with the eggplants. Continue baking until the eggplants and garlic are tender, about 20 minutes. Remove from the oven and let cool. Scrape out the meat of the eggplant and discard the skins.

In a large pot, combine 1 teaspoon olive oil and onion over medium-high heat. Cook until tender, about 7 minutes. Add eggplant, garlic, vegetable broth, tomato purée and red pepper flakes. Bring to a boil over medium-high heat. Reduce the heat to medium-low and cover, simmering for 30 minutes.

In batches, pour the mixture into a blender and purée. Return to the pot and stir in cream. Season with salt and pepper. Cook over low heat until slightly thickened and serve.

MINESTRA DI PISELLI
GREEN PEA SOUP
SERVES 4

INGREDIENTS

1/4 CUP EXTRA-VIRGIN OLIVE OIL

1 CUP DICED CELERY

1 CUP CHOPPED GREEN ONIONS

4 CUPS VEGETABLE BROTH
  (PAGE 68)

1 CUP ENGLISH PEAS

1 LEMON, ZESTED

3 BASIL LEAVES

SALT AND PEPPER

INSTRUCTIONS

In a medium pot, heat olive oil over medium heat until shimmering. Add celery and green onions, cooking until translucent, about 5 minutes. Add vegetable broth and bring to a boil. Add peas, lemon zest and basil leaves. Bring to a boil.

Remove from the heat. Purée in a food processor until smooth. Season with salt and pepper and chill.

ZUPPA DI CINGHIALE
WILD BOAR SOUP
SERVES 6

INGREDIENTS

2 TABLESPOONS EXTRA-VIRGIN
  OLIVE OIL

1 LARGE WHITE ONION, CHOPPED

1 TABLESPOON MINCED GARLIC

1 1/2 POUNDS WILD BOAR
  SHOULDER, CUT INTO
  SMALL PIECES

1 CUP RED TABLE WINE

2 TEASPOONS FRESH BASIL

2 TEASPOONS FRESH OREGANO

1 CAN (28 OUNCES) SAN MARZANO
  TOMATOES

12 SAGE LEAVES

1 CUP DRIED CANNELLINI BEANS

1 CARROT, CHOPPED

1 ZUCCHINI, CHOPPED

1 CUP GREEN BEANS CUT IN
  BITE-SIZE PIECES

1 CUP WATER

8 OUNCES FUSILLI PASTA

PARMIGIANO-REGGIANO

SALT AND PEPPER

INSTRUCTIONS

In a large skillet, heat olive oil over medium heat until shimmering. Add onion and garlic, and cook until the onion is translucent. Add wild boar and cook for 5 minutes. Add wine, basil, oregano, salt and pepper. Bring to a boil. Reduce the heat to medium-low and simmer, covered, for 30 minutes.

Add tomatoes and smash with a spoon. Add sage, cannellini beans, carrot, zucchini and green beans. Simmer, covered, for 1 1/2 hours, stirring occasionally.

Add water and pasta to the skillet, cooking until tender. Spoon into individual bowls and top with Parmigiano-Reggiano.

BRODO DI PESCE/VEGETALE
FISH/VEGETABLE* BROTH
MAKES 4 QUARTS

INGREDIENTS

2 POUNDS FISH HEADS, FISH
  STRIPS, PRAWN SHELLS OR
  WHOLE FISH
2 CELERY STALKS, BROKEN
  INTO PIECES
2 CARROTS, PEELED, CUT IN HALF
1 LARGE ONION, QUARTERED
6 BLACK PEPPERCORNS
2 TABLESPOONS SALT
3 BAY LEAVES, BROKEN INTO
  SMALL PIECES
2 TABLESPOONS LOBSTER BASE
  (OPTIONAL)
4 QUARTS PLUS 2 CUPS
  COLD WATER

INSTRUCTIONS

In a large pot, place seafood, celery, carrots, onion, peppercorns, salt, bay leaves and lobster base. Add cold water and simmer, uncovered, over medium-low heat for 1 hour. Skim the surface foam occasionally with a slotted spoon.

Strain the broth, discarding the solids.

*For vegetable broth, omit the seafood and lobster base.

BRODO DI POLLO
CHICKEN BROTH
MAKES 4 QUARTS

INGREDIENTS

1 CHICKEN (4 POUNDS), CUT
  INTO 6 PIECES
2 CELERY STALKS, BROKEN
  INTO PIECES
2 CARROTS, PEELED, CUT IN HALF
1 LARGE ONION, QUARTERED
6 BLACK PEPPERCORNS
2 TABLESPOONS SALT
3 BAY LEAVES, BROKEN INTO
  SMALL PIECES
2 TABLESPOONS CHICKEN BASE
  (OPTIONAL)
4 QUARTS PLUS 2 CUPS
  COLD WATER

INSTRUCTIONS

In a large pot, place chicken pieces, celery, carrots, onion, peppercorns, salt, bay leaves and chicken base. Add cold water and simmer, uncovered, over medium-low heat for 3 hours.

Strain the broth, discarding the solids.

PASTA

THE SWEETNESS OF THE CREAM BALANCES THE SALT OF THE SMOKED SALMON, A PERFECT MARRIAGE IN YOUR MOUTH.

TAGLIATELLE CON SALMONE AFFUMICATO
PASTA WITH SMOKED SALMON
SERVES 4

INGREDIENTS

1 POUND TAGLIATELLE
4 CUPS HEAVY CREAM
1/4 CUP UNSALTED BUTTER
1 POUND SMOKED SALMON, DICED
1/4 CUP CHOPPED FRESH CHIVES
1/4 CUP OIL-PACKED SUN-DRIED
  TOMATO HALVES, DRAINED,
  CHOPPED
2 TABLESPOONS CHOPPED FRESH
  PARSLEY
SALT AND PEPPER

INSTRUCTIONS

In a large pot, bring 6 quarts of salted water to a boil. Add tagliatelle and cook until al dente. Drain the pasta.

In a large saucepan over medium heat, combine cream and butter. Cook until reduced by half. Add salmon, chives, sun-dried tomatoes, salt and pepper. Cook for 1 minute, stirring continuously. Add the tagliatelle to the pan and toss to coat. Garnish with parsley and serve.

LINGUINE CON LE VONGOLE

PASTA WITH CLAMS

SERVES 4

INGREDIENTS

- 1 POUND LINGUINE
- 3 TABLESPOONS EXTRA-VIRGIN OLIVE OIL
- 4 CLOVES GARLIC, MINCED
- 1 POUND MANILA CLAMS, SCRUBBED, RINSED
- 1/2 CUP DRY WHITE WINE
- 1 CUP DICED PLUM TOMATOES
- 1/4 TEASPOON CRUSHED RED PEPPER FLAKES
- 1/2 CUP CHOPPED FRESH ITALIAN PARSLEY

INSTRUCTIONS

In a large pot, bring 6 quarts of salted water to a boil. Add linguine and cook until al dente. Drain the pasta, reserving 1 cup cooked pasta water.

In a large skillet, heat olive oil over medium heat until shimmering. Add garlic and cook until golden brown. Add clams, wine, tomatoes and red pepper flakes. Cover and cook for 8 minutes, or until the clams have opened. Toss out any unopened clams.

Add the pasta to the skillet and stir in parsley. Add the desired amount of reserved pasta water if the linguine is too dry. Serve.

PAGLIA E FIENO TRANSLATES TO "STRAW AND HAY," REFERRING TO THE DIFFERENT COLORS OF PASTA, A PERFECT FALL DISH.

PAGLIA E FIENO
GREEN PEA PASTA
SERVES 4

INGREDIENTS

1/2 POUND SPINACH FETTUCCINE

1/2 POUND FETTUCCINE

1 TABLESPOON EXTRA-VIRGIN
   OLIVE OIL

1/2 CUP DICED PROSCIUTTO

1 CUP HEAVY CREAM

1 CUP GREEN PEAS

2/3 CUP GRATED PARMIGIANO-
   REGGIANO

1/4 TEASPOON GRATED NUTMEG

SALT AND PEPPER

INSTRUCTIONS

In a large pot, bring 6 quarts of salted water to a boil. Add fettuccine and cook until al dente. Drain the pasta.

In a large saucepan over medium heat, heat olive oil until shimmering. Add prosciutto and cook until browned. Add cream and bring to a boil. Simmer for 2 minutes, until slightly thickened. Add pasta, peas and cheese. Season with salt, pepper and nutmeg. Stir to coat the pasta and cook for 3 minutes. Remove from the heat and serve.

THIS IS AN EXTREMELY TRADITIONAL ROMAN DISH. MAKE ONLY WITH CHEESE AND BLACK PEPPER. SO SIMPLE YET AT SAME TIME SO POWERFUL. USING ONLY HIGH-QUALITY INGREDIENTS IS THE KEY.

CACIO E PEPE
CHEESE AND PEPPER PASTA
SERVES 4

INGREDIENTS

- 1 POUND SPAGHETTI
- 2 TABLESPOONS EXTRA-VIRGIN OLIVE OIL
- 2 TEASPOONS GROUND BLACK PEPPER
- 3/4 CUP GRATED PARMIGIANO-REGGIANO
- 1/3 CUP GRATED PECORINO

INSTRUCTIONS

In a large pot, bring 6 quarts of salted water to a boil. Add spaghetti and cook until al dente. Drain the pasta and reserve 1/2 cup cooked pasta water.

In a large sauté pan, heat 1 tablespoon olive oil over medium heat. Add pepper and cook for 1 minute. Add reserved pasta water and bring to a simmer. Add the pasta, remaining olive oil and Parmigiano-Reggiano. Reduce the heat to low and stir until the cheese is melted. Remove from the heat and add the Pecorino. Stir until the cheese melts and serve.

ORECCHIETTE FILOSOFO
PASTA WITH ITALIAN SAUSAGE AND BROCCOLI
SERVES 4

INGREDIENTS

1 POUND FRESH BROCCOLI

1 POUND ORECCHIETTE PASTA

3 TABLESPOONS EXTRA-VIRGIN
OLIVE OIL

1 POUND BULK MILD ITALIAN
SAUSAGE

3 CLOVES GARLIC, MINCED

1 PINCH CRUSHED RED PEPPER
FLAKES

1 CUP PITTED KALAMATA OLIVES,
SLICED

1/4 CUP GRATED PECORINO
ROMANO

SALT

INSTRUCTIONS

In a large pot, bring 6 quarts of salted water to a boil. Using a knife, separate the broccolli florets from the stems and add the stems to the boiling water. After 3 minutes, add the florets and cook for another 5 minutes, or until tender. Using a slotted spoon, transfer the broccoli to a bowl of ice water, saving the cooking water.

Reheat the cooking water and bring to a boil. Add orecchiette and cook until al dente. Drain the pasta.

In a large skillet, heat olive oil over medium heat until shimmering. Add sausage and break into pieces, cooking until golden brown, about 8 minutes. Add garlic and red pepper flakes, sautéing for 3 minutes.

Strain the broccoli and add to the sausage mixture. Add the pasta and olives. Stir in Pecorino Romano and serve.

FETTUCCINE CON GAMBERI
PASTA WITH SHRIMP
SERVES 4

INGREDIENTS

1 POUND FETTUCCINE

2 TABLESPOONS EXTRA-VIRGIN
   OLIVE OIL

1/2 SMALL WHITE ONION, CHOPPED

2 CLOVES GARLIC, MINCED

1/2 CUP CHARDONNAY

1 CUP MARINARA (PAGE 94)

1 POUND MEDIUM SHRIMP,
   SHELLED, DEVEINED

INSTRUCTIONS

In a large pot, bring 6 quarts of salted water to a boil. Add fettuccine and cook until al dente. Drain the pasta, reserving 1/4 cup cooked pasta water.

In a large sauté pan, heat olive oil over medium heat until shimmering. Add onion and cook until translucent. Add garlic and cook, stirring, for 30 seconds. Add wine and cook until evaporated. Stir in marinara. Add shrimp and cook for 3 minutes, or until pink. Add the pasta and cooked pasta water, tossing until combined. Serve.

THE KEY TO ITALIAN COOKING IS FRESHNESS AND INGREDIENTS. WHEN SARDINES ARE NOT IN SEASON, USE TUNA PACKED IN WATER. ALWAYS PAY ATTENTION TO THE SEASONAL INGREDIENTS.

SPAGHETTI CON SARDINE
PASTA WITH SARDINES AND BREAD CRUMBS
SERVES 4

INGREDIENTS

1 POUND SPAGHETTI

1/4 CUP PLUS 3 TABLESPOONS
   EXTRA-VIRGIN OLIVE OIL

8 CLOVES GARLIC, CHOPPED

1 1/2 CUPS DRIED BREAD CRUMBS

1/2 CUP CHOPPED FRESH PARSLEY

8 OUNCES FRESH SARDINES,
   CHOPPED

1 TEASPOON CRUSHED RED
   PEPPER FLAKES

1 CUP DRIED CURRANTS

SALT AND PEPPER

INSTRUCTIONS

In a large pot, bring 6 quarts of salted water to a boil. Add spaghetti and cook until al dente. Drain the pasta.

In a large skillet over medium heat, heat 1/4 cup olive oil until shimmering. Add garlic and cook for 30 seconds. Add bread crumbs and cook until golden brown, stirring constantly. Add parsley, salt and pepper. Transfer the bread mixture to a medium bowl and set aside.

Return the skillet to medium heat and add remaining olive oil. Add sardines, red pepper flakes and currants. Sauté for 3 minutes. Add the pasta and toss with the sardine mixture. Add the bread mixture to the pan and stir to combine. Serve.

FUSILLI ZAFFERANO
PASTA WITH SAFFRON
SERVES 4

INGREDIENTS

1 POUND FUSILLI

2 TABLESPOONS EXTRA-VIRGIN
OLIVE OIL

12 OUNCES BULK ITALIAN SAUSAGE

2 TABLESPOONS PINE NUTS

2 TABLESPOONS DRIED CURRANTS

1 OUNCE SAFFRON TEA

1 CUP HEAVY CREAM

2 CUPS ARUGULA

1/4 CUP PLUS 1/4 CUP GRATED
PECORINO ROMANO

SALT AND PEPPER

SAFFRON TEA

1 TABLESPOON SAFFRON THREADS

3 CUPS COLD WATER

INSTRUCTIONS

In a large pot, bring 6 quarts of salted water to a boil. Add fusilli and cook until al dente. Drain the pasta.

In a large sauté pan, heat olive oil over medium heat until shimmering. Add sausage, breaking into small pieces, and cook until browned. Add pine nuts and sauté for 1 minute. Stir in currants and saffron tea. Add cream, salt and pepper. Cook until fairly thick. Add arugula, 1/4 cup Pecorino Romano and pasta. Cook, stirring, until the arugula is slightly wilted. Garnish with the remaining cheese and serve.

SAFFRON TEA

Heat a small frying pan over medium-low heat. Add saffron threads and toast for 4 minutes, stirring often. The saffron should not turn black. Remove the saffron from the pan.

In a medium saucepan, bring water to a boil. Add saffron and reduce the heat to low. Simmer for 10 minutes. You can either strain the tea or leave the threads in the liquid.

GNOCCHI
RICOTTA GNOCCHI
SERVES 6

INGREDIENTS

8 OUNCES RICOTTA
1 MEDIUM ONION, CHOPPED
1 LARGE EGG
1 EGG YOLK
1/2 CUP PLUS 1/2 CUP GRATED
  PARMIGIANO-REGGIANO
1 CUP ALL-PURPOSE FLOUR
4 TABLESPOONS UNSALTED
  BUTTER
4 SAGE LEAVES
EXTRA-VIRGIN OLIVE OIL
SALT AND PEPPER

INSTRUCTIONS

In a large bowl, combine ricotta, onion, egg, yolk, 1/2 cup Parmigiano-Reggiano, salt and pepper. Mix thoroughly with a fork until smooth.

Roll the mixture into tablespoon-sized balls. Coat lightly with flour.

In a small saucepan, heat butter and sage over medium heat. Turn off the heat and let stand.

In a large pot, bring 6 quarts of salted water to a boil. Add a few drops of olive oil. Add the dumplings and when they float on the surface, remove with a slotted spoon to serving plates. Drizzle with sage-butter sauce and sprinkle with the remaining Parmigiano-Reggiano.

CAPELLINI AI GRANCHI
PASTA WITH CRAB
SERVES 4

INGREDIENTS

1 POUND CAPELLINI

2 TEASPOONS EXTRA-VIRGIN
OLIVE OIL

3 CLOVES GARLIC, DICED

1 TEASPOON CHOPPED FRESH
ROSEMARY

6 GREEN ONIONS, CHOPPED

4 ROMA TOMATOES, DICED

1 CUP DRY WHITE WINE

1/2 POUND CRABMEAT

1 CUP FISH BROTH (PAGE 68)

1/4 CUP CHOPPED FRESH ITALIAN
PARSLEY

SALT AND PEPPER

INSTRUCTIONS

In a large pot, bring 6 quarts of salted water to a boil. Add capellini and cook until al dente. Drain the pasta.

In a medium sauté pan, heat olive oil over medium heat. Add garlic, rosemary and onions. Cook until the garlic is golden brown. Stir in tomatoes and wine. Bring to a boil. Add crab, fish broth, parsley, salt and pepper. Reduce the heat and simmer for 6 minutes. Add the pasta and stir to coat. Garnish with parsley and serve.

THIS IS A VERY TRADITIONAL DISH FROM ROME. IT IS A SIMPLE RECIPE THAT MAKES YOU HAPPY ANY TIME OF THE YEAR AND MATCHES WITH ALL KINDS OF WINES. THE PERFECT SPICE.

LINGUINE ALL'AMATRICIANA

PASTA WITH PANCETTA AND TOMATOES
SERVES 4

INGREDIENTS

- 1 POUND LINGUINE
- 2 TABLESPOONS EXTRA-VIRGIN OLIVE OIL
- 1/2 POUND PANCETTA, DICED
- 1 SMALL WHITE ONION, DICED
- 1 CAN (28 OUNCES) SAN MARZANO TOMATOES
- 1/4 CUP GRATED PECORINO ROMANO
- 2 TEASPOONS CRUSHED RED PEPPER FLAKES
- 1 TABLESPOON GROUND BLACK PEPPER

INSTRUCTIONS

In a large pot, bring 6 quarts of salted water to a boil. Add linguine and cook until al dente. Drain the pasta.

In a large sauté pan, heat olive oil over high heat until shimmering. Add pancetta and cook until the fat has been rendered from the meat. Turn the heat down to medium. Add onions and cook until translucent. Add tomatoes and mash with a spoon. Cook for 1 minute. Stir in cheese, red pepper flakes and black pepper. Turn the heat to low. Add the pasta to the sauce and serve.

AT THE END OF SUMMER, ARTICHOKES ARE BLOOMING. THE SIMPLICITY OF THE EARTH IS ALL AROUND AND YOU WANT TO BE CLOSE TO THE EARTH. THIS DISH GIVES A SALUTE AND WELCOMES THE FALL.

PENNE AI CARCIOFI
PASTA WITH ARTICHOKES
SERVES 4

INGREDIENTS

1 POUND PENNE

2 TABLESPOONS EXTRA-VIRGIN
   OLIVE OIL

1 MEDIUM WHITE ONION,
   CHOPPED

3 OUNCES PANCETTA, DICED

1 CAN (28 OUNCES) ARTICHOKE
   HEARTS, DRAINED, DICED

2 LARGE EGGS

2 TABLESPOONS GRATED
   PARMIGIANO-REGGIANO

1/4 CUP CHOPPED FRESH PARSLEY

SALT AND PEPPER

INSTRUCTIONS

In a large pot, bring 6 quarts of salted water to a boil. Add penne and cook until al dente. Drain the pasta.

In a large sauté pan, heat olive oil over medium heat until shimmering. Add onion and pancetta, and cook until the onion is translucent. Add artichokes. Cover and let simmer for 10 minutes.

In a small bowl, whisk eggs and cheese. Remove the artichoke mixture from the pan and place in a medium bowl. Slowly stir the egg mixture into the artichokes, making sure not to scramble the eggs. Add the pasta and pepper to taste to the artichoke mixture and toss to blend. Garnish wtih parsley and serve.

MARINARA
TOMATO SAUCE
MAKES 6 CUPS

INGREDIENTS

2 TABLESPOONS EXTRA-VIRGIN
   OLIVE OIL
3/4 CUP CHOPPED YELLOW ONION
2 CLOVES GARLIC, CHOPPED
1 CUP DRY WHITE WINE
2 CANS (28 OUNCES) PLUM
   TOMATOES, WHOLE, PEELED
1 CARROT, PEELED, QUARTERED
1 CELERY STALK, HALVED
1/2 TEASPOON SALT
1/2 TEASPOON GROUND
   BLACK PEPPER
6 BASIL LEAVES

INSTRUCTIONS

In a medium sauté pan, heat olive oil over medium heat until shimmering. Add onion and sauté until translucent. Add garlic and sauté until golden brown. Add wine and simmer until the liquid is reduced by half.

Pour in tomatoes and mash with a spoon. Bring to a boil. Bundle the carrot and celery, tying with kitchen string. Add to the sauce. Stir in salt and pepper and reduce the heat to low, simmering for 20 minutes. Add basil leaves and continue simmering for 10 minutes. Remove the carrot and celery. Serve.

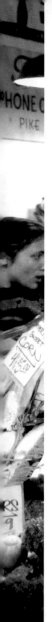

RISOTTO

RISOTTO CON SALSICCIA ITALIANA
RISOTTO WITH ITALIAN SAUSAGE **99**

RISOTTO CON FRUTTI DI MARE
SEAFOOD RISOTTO **101**

RISOTTO SIENESE
PROSCIUTTO AND GORGONZOLA RISOTTO **104**

RISOTTO AL POMODORO E CARNE
TOMATO AND FILET MIGNON RISOTTO **105**

RISOTTO
BASIC RISOTTO **106**

RISOTTO CON SALSICCIA ITALIANA
RISOTTO WITH ITALIAN SAUSAGE
SERVES 6

INGREDIENTS

1 TABLESPOON EXTRA-VIRGIN
   OLIVE OIL
16 OUNCES MILD ITALIAN SAUSAGE,
   GROUND OR SLICED
1 CUP DICED WHITE ONION
1 TABLESPOON MINCED GARLIC
1/2 TEASPOON DRIED THYME
2 CUPS ARBORIO RICE
1 CUP DRY WHITE WINE
1 CUP CHICKEN BROTH (PAGE 69)
2 CUPS WATER
1 CUP GREEN PEAS
1/4 CUP GRATED PARMIGIANO-
   REGGIANO
2 TABLESPOONS CHOPPED FRESH
   PARSLEY
SALT AND PEPPER

INSTRUCTIONS

In a large sauté pan, heat olive oil over medium heat until shimmering. Add sausage and onion, and sauté until the onion is translucent. Add garlic and thyme, and cook until the garlic turns golden brown. Add rice and wine, and stir for 2 minutes, or until the wine is absorbed. Stir in broth and 1 cup water, and lower the heat to medium-low. Simmer until the broth is absorbed, stirring constantly, about 15 minutes.

Add the remaining water and continue stirring until the liquid is absorbed, about 6 minutes. Stir in peas and cheese, and cook for 1 minute. Season with salt and pepper. Garnish with parsley and serve.

RISOTTO CON FRUTTI DI MARE

SEAFOOD RISOTTO

SERVES 6

INGREDIENTS

7 TABLESPOONS UNSALTED
  BUTTER
1 CUP DICED WHITE ONION
2 CUPS ARBORIO RICE
1 CUP DRY WHITE WINE
2 CUPS WATER
1 TEASPOON CHOPPED GARLIC
1 CUP FISH BROTH (PAGE 68)
2 POUNDS MUSSELS, CLAMS,
  OCTOPUS OR SALMON, CLEANED,
  TRIMMED, DICED
1/4 CUP HEAVY CREAM
1/2 CUP GRATED PARMIGIANO-
  REGGIANO
3 TABLESPOONS CHOPPED GREEN
  ONIONS, GREEN PART ONLY
2 TABLESPOONS CHOPPED FRESH
  PARSLEY
SALT AND PEPPER

INSTRUCTIONS

In a large sauté pan, melt 3 tablespoons butter over medium heat. Add onion and sauté until translucent. Add rice and stir constantly for 3 minutes. Add wine, 1 cup water and garlic. Continue to stir and cook until all liquid is absorbed. Add remaining water and repeat the previous step. Add broth, salt, pepper and 3 tablespoons butter. Simmer on medium-low heat for 12 minutes, stirring constantly.

Season seafood with salt and pepper, and add to the rice mixture. Cook for 6 minutes over medium-low heat. Stir in remaining butter, cream, cheese and green onions. Simmer for 2 minutes, stirring constantly. Remove from the heat and discard any mussels and clams that are unopened. Garnish with parsley and serve.

RISOTTO SIENESE
PROSCIUTTO AND GORGONZOLA RISOTTO
SERVES 4

INGREDIENTS

1 1/2 TABLESPOONS UNSALTED
   BUTTER
4 OUNCES PROSCIUTTO, DICED
1/2 CUP DRY WHITE WINE
3 CUPS CHICKEN BROTH (PAGE 69)
2 CUPS HEAVY CREAM
1/2 CUP CRUMBLED GORGONZOLA
2 CUPS ARBORIO RICE
1 CUP GREEN PEAS
1/2 CUP GRATED PARMIGIANO-
   REGGIANO
SALT AND PEPPER

INSTRUCTIONS

In a large sauté pan, melt butter over medium heat. Add prosciutto, salt and pepper. Sauté for 2 minutes. Add wine, chicken broth and cream. Increase the heat to medium-high and bring to a boil, stirring occasionally, for 5 minutes. Add Gorgonzola and stir until melted.

Reduce the heat to medium-low and add rice. Simmer for 15 minutes, stirring often. Add peas and continue to stir until the liquid is mostly cooked out and the rice has a creamy texture. Stir in Parmigiano-Reggiano and serve.

RISOTTO AL POMODORO E CARNE
TOMATO AND FILET MIGNON RISOTTO
SERVES 4

INGREDIENTS

2 TABLESPOONS EXTRA-VIRGIN
OLIVE OIL

1 TABLESPOON UNSALTED BUTTER

2 CLOVES GARLIC, MINCED

1 SMALL WHITE ONION, CHOPPED

12 OUNCES FILET MIGNON, DICED

2 CUPS ARBORIO RICE

3/4 CUP RED TABLE WINE

1 1/2 CUPS CHICKEN BROTH
(PAGE 69)

1 CAN (14 OUNCES) SAN MARZANO
TOMATOES, CRUSHED

1/2 CUP WATER

1/2 CUP PLUS 1/4 CUP GRATED
PARMIGIANO-REGGIANO

1 TABLESPOON CHOPPED FRESH
ITALIAN PARSLEY

1 TABLESPOON CHOPPED FRESH
BASIL

SALT AND PEPPER

INSTRUCTIONS

In a large sauté pan, heat olive oil and butter over high heat. Add garlic and cook until the butter browns. Add onion and cook until translucent. Reduce the heat to low and add filet. Cook for 3 minutes.

Stir in rice and increase the heat to medium. Cook, stirring constantly, until the rice browns. Add wine and stir until the liquid is absorbed. Add chicken broth 1/2 cup at a time. Cook, stirring constantly, until the liquid is completely absorbed before adding more.

Add tomatoes and mash with a spoon. Season with salt and pepper. Stir in water. Once the water is absorbed, stir in 1/2 cup cheese. Continue stirring for about 2 minutes, or until the rice has a creamy texture. Let the risotto sit for 3 minutes, then transfer to a serving bowl. Garnish with remaining cheese, parsley and basil.

RISOTTO
BASIC RISOTTO
SERVES 6

INGREDIENTS

6 TABLESPOONS UNSALTED
  BUTTER
1 CUP DICED WHITE ONION
2 CUPS ARBORIO RICE
1 CUP DRY WHITE WINE
2 CUPS WATER
1 CUP BROTH (PAGE 68, 69)
1 TEASPOON SALT
1 TEASPOON GROUND BLACK
  PEPPER

INSTRUCTIONS

In a large sauté pan, melt 3 tablespoons butter over medium heat. Add onion and sauté until translucent. Add rice and stir constantly for 3 minutes. Add wine and 1 cup water. Continue to stir and cook until all the liquid is absorbed. Add remaining water and repeat the previous step. Add broth, salt, pepper and remaining butter. Simmer until the rice is cooked and has a creamy texture, about 15 minutes.

PIATTO FORTE

MELANZANE AL FORNO
EGGPLANT PARMESAN **110**

POLPETTONE ITALIANO
ITALIAN MEATLOAF **111**

BRASATO DI CARNE AL CHIANTI
CHIANTI BRAISED BEEF **115**

COTOLETTA ALLA VALDOSTANA
VEAL CHOPS **116**

BRASATO DI PANCETTA
MUSTARD BRAISED PORK BELLY **117**

BRACIOLA CON ROSMARINO
PORCHETTA WITH ROSEMARY **119**

IPPOGLOSSO AL VAPORE
STEAMED HALIBUT **121**

BRANZINO
ROASTED BRANZINO WITH LEMONS **124**

TAGLIATA CON RUCOLA
SIRLOIN WITH ARUGULA **125**

GUANCIALE DI MANZO
BAROLO BRAISED BEEF CHEEKS **127**

BRASATO DI POLLO
TOMATO AND WINE BRAISED CHICKEN **129**

MELANZANE AL FORNO
EGGPLANT PARMESAN
SERVES 6

INGREDIENTS

6 MEDIUM EGGPLANTS
VEGETABLE OIL
2 CUPS ALL-PURPOSE FLOUR
2 EGGS
2 CUPS HEAVY CREAM
2 CUPS PANKO CRUMBS
2 CUPS MARINARA (PAGE 94)
2 CUPS PLUS 1/2 CUP GRATED
   PECORINO ROMANO
2 CUPS SHREDDED MOZZARELLA
1 BUNCH BASIL, CHOPPED
SALT AND PEPPER

INSTRUCTIONS

Preheat oven to 350°F.

Slice eggplants horizontally about 1/4 inch thick and season with salt and pepper.

Fill a large pot 1/3 full of vegetable oil and heat over medium-high heat to 350°F. Pour flour into a medium bowl. Whisk eggs in another medium bowl. Combine cream, salt and pepper in a separate medium bowl. Place panko in another medium bowl. Dip each eggplant slice in the following order: flour, eggwash, cream and panko. Deep-fry eggplant slices in small batches until golden brown and let dry on a paper towel.

In a large casserole dish, spread 1/2 cup marinara on the bottom. Sprinkle with 1/2 cup Pecorino Romano, 1/2 cup mozzarella and 1/4 of the basil. Top with eggplant slices in a single layer. Repeat the layering process until all the ingredients have been used, finishing with Pecorino Romano.

Bake for 15 minutes, or golden brown and the cheese has melted. Serve.

THIS DISH WAS MY FIRST EXPERIENCE WITH FOOD NETWORK. THIS IS A GREAT MEMORY DISH FOR ME. AS YOU MAY KNOW, WE DON'T HAVE MEATLOAF IN ITALY, BUT I CREATED THIS HUMBLE RECIPE TO LIFT THE SPIRITS, A FEEL-GOOD DISH.

POLPETTONE ITALIANO
ITALIAN MEATLOAF
SERVES 8

INGREDIENTS

1/4 CUP PLUS 2 TABLESPOONS EXTRA-VIRGIN OLIVE OIL

5 CLOVES GARLIC, CHOPPED

2 RED BELL PEPPERS, SEEDED, DICED

2 MEDIUM YELLOW ONIONS, DICED

1/2 CUP PINE NUTS

1/2 CUP CHOPPED FRESH BASIL LEAVES

2 TABLESPOONS CHOPPED FRESH PARSLEY

4 LARGE EGGS

2 CUPS GRATED PARMIGIANO-REGGIANO

1 1/2 CUPS DRIED BREAD CRUMBS

3 POUNDS GROUND BEEF

2 TABLESPOONS BALSAMIC VINEGAR

1 CUP MARINARA (PAGE 94)

SALT AND PEPPER

INSTRUCTIONS

Preheat oven to 350°F.

In a large sauté pan, heat 1/4 cup olive oil over medium heat until shimmering. Add garlic and sauté for 1 minute. Add peppers, onions and pine nuts. Sauté until the onions are translucent.

In a small bowl, combine basil, parsley and eggs. Add salt and pepper. In another small bowl, combine Parmigiano-Reggiano and bread crumbs. In a large bowl, combine meat, egg mixture, bread mixture, onion mixture, vinegar and remaining olive oil with your hands.

In an oiled loaf pan, pack the meat mixture. Top with marinara. Bake for 60 minutes, or until the internal temperature is 170°F. Remove from the oven and let rest for 5 minutes. Cut into 2-inch slices and serve.

THIS IS A DISH YOU HAVE TO MAKE ON A DARK DAY OF WINTER. IT'S A HEAVY DISH THAT NEEDS THE EARLY DARKNESS TO ENJOY. LET IT COOK ALL DAY, EAT EARLY, AND HAVE ALL NIGHT TO DIGEST. IT'S CRIMINAL IF YOU EAT THIS DISH IN THE SUMMERTIME!

BRASATO DI CARNE AL CHIANTI
CHIANTI BRAISED BEEF
SERVES 8

INGREDIENTS

6-POUND BONELESS BOTTOM
   RUMP BEEF ROAST, TRIMMED

1/2 CUP EXTRA-VIRGIN OLIVE OIL

3 SMALL WHITE ONIONS, PEELED,
   QUARTERED

6 CARROTS, PEELED, CHOPPED
   INTO WEDGES

5 CELERY STALKS, CHOPPED
   INTO WEDGES

10 CLOVES GARLIC, PEELED

1/4 BUNCH ROSEMARY

8 SAGE LEAVES

1/2 TEASPOON GRATED NUTMEG

1 TEASPOON WHOLE BLACK
   PEPPERCORNS

1 CUP PORCINI MUSHROOMS,
   SLICED

3 BOTTLES CHIANTI

3 CUPS VEGETABLE BROTH
   (PAGE 68)

SALT

INSTRUCTIONS

Preheat oven to 250°F. Season the outside of the roast with salt. In a large ovenproof saucepan or Dutch oven, heat olive oil over medium heat until shimmering.

Place the roast in the pan and brown each side for 2 minutes, or until caramelized. Move the roast to a platter. In the pan with oil, toss onions, carrots, celery and garlic. Add rosemary, sage, nutmeg, peppercorns, mushrooms and salt. Cook over medium heat for 4 minutes, or until the vegetables soften. Make sure to scrape the browned bits from the bottom and stir frequently. Reduce the heat, pushing the vegetables to the side of the pan.

Place the roast in the center. Pour in wine and meat juices from the platter. The roast should be half submerged. Add broth as needed. Cover and turn the heat to high until the liquid is steaming. Uncover and place the pan in the oven. Cook for 30 minutes and then rotate the roast. Turn the meat every 30 minutes for 3 hours. The liquid should not boil. If it does, lower the temperature and add cold water to stop.

After 4 1/2 hours, use a meat thermometer to check the temperature in the center of the roast. Once it reads 180°F, remove the pan from the oven. Place the meat on a serving tray and garnish with carrots, celery and juices. Serve.

COTOLETTA ALLA VALDOSTANA
VEAL CHOPS
SERVES 4

INGREDIENTS

4 VEAL CHOPS, 1 1/2 INCHES THICK

4 SLICES PROSCIUTTO

8 SAGE LEAVES

8 SLICES FONTINA

3 TABLESPOONS EXTRA-VIRGIN
   OLIVE OIL

1/4 CUP CHARDONNAY

1 CUP CHICKEN BROTH (PAGE 69)

1 LEMON, QUARTERED

SALT AND PEPPER

INSTRUCTIONS

Preheat oven to 350°F.

Using a knife, cut a 2 1/2-inch-deep, 1-inch-wide horizontal pocket into the center of each chop. Lay out the prosciutto slices. On one end, place 1 sage leaf and 2 slices of cheese. Starting at the same end, roll the prosciutto into a tube and insert into each veal chop. Seal the chops with toothpicks. Season the chops lightly with salt and pepper.

In a large ovenproof skillet, heat olive oil over medium heat until shimmering. Add the veal chops and cook for 4 minutes on each side. Place the skillet in the oven and cook until the internal temperature of each chop is 140°F, about 12 minutes. Remove the chops from the oven and let rest for 5 minutes on a cutting board. Reserve the pan and juices.

Set the skillet over medium-high heat. Add remaining sage leaves and cook for 1 minute. Deglaze the pan with wine and reduce for 1 minute. Add broth and reduce for 2 minutes. Season with salt and pepper. Transfer the veal chops to plates and pour the sauce over the chops. Serve with lemon wedges.

BRASATO DI PANCETTA
MUSTARD BRAISED PORK BELLY
SERVES 8

INGREDIENTS

3 POUNDS PORK BELLY,
  SKIN REMOVED
EXTRA-VIRGIN OLIVE OIL
1 SMALL WHITE ONION, CHOPPED
1/2 FENNEL BULB, MIDDLE
  REMOVED, CHOPPED
2 CLOVES GARLIC, SMASHED
1 CUP CHARDONNAY
1/4 CUP STONE-GROUND MUSTARD
3 CUPS CHICKEN BROTH (PAGE 69)
1 BUNCH THYME, SEPARATED
4 BAY LEAVES
SALT AND PEPPER

RUB

2 TABLESPOONS MUSTARD
  POWDER
2 TABLESPOONS MUSTARD SEEDS
GRATED ZEST OF 1 ORANGE
2 SPRIGS ROSEMARY, CHOPPED
2 CLOVES GARLIC, SMASHED
1 TABLESPOON DRIED OREGANO
2 TABLESPOONS KOSHER SALT
1 TABLESPOON BLACK PEPPER

INSTRUCTIONS

In a large bowl, combine all ingredients for the rub. Massage into the pork belly. Cover with plastic and refrigerate for 12 hours.

Preheat oven to 325°F. Coat a straight-sided pan with olive oil and heat over medium heat. Add onion, fennel and garlic. Season with salt and cook until soft, about 8 minutes. Add wine and cook for 3 minutes. Stir in mustard and 2 cups chicken broth. Add pork belly, thyme and bay leaves. Season with pepper. Cover the pan and place in the oven. Braise for 6 hours, occasionally rotating the pan. If the liquid level drops, add remaining broth.

Remove the pan lid and turn the oven to broil. Cook until the pork belly turns golden, about 2 minutes. Transfer the pork belly to a cutting board. Slice and arrange on a serving platter. Ladle the braising juices on top and serve.

BRACIOLA CON ROSMARINO
PORCHETTA WITH ROSEMARY
SERVES 8

INGREDIENTS

1 BUNCH ROSEMARY, CHOPPED

1 BUNCH SAGE, CHOPPED

10 CLOVES GARLIC, MINCED

1 TABLESPOON CRUSHED RED
   PEPPER FLAKES

1/4 CUP PLUS 2 TABLESPOONS
   EXTRA-VIRGIN OLIVE OIL

1 PICNIC (LOWER) SHOULDER OF
   PORK, SKIN AND BONE REMOVED

4 CUPS DRY WHITE WINE

1 BUNCH THYME

10 BAY LEAVES

4 CUPS CHICKEN BROTH (PAGE 69)

SALT AND PEPPER

VEGETABLES

2 MEDIUM ONIONS, DICED

10 CLOVES GARLIC, SMASHED

1 POUND RED POTATOES,
   CUT IN HALF

2 CUPS CHOPPED BROCCOLI

2 LARGE CARROTS, PEELED, DICED
   INTO 1/2-INCH PIECES

INSTRUCTIONS

Preheat oven to 450°F.

In a medium bowl, combine rosemary, sage, garlic and red pepper. Mix with 1/4 cup olive oil. Gently cut the sides of the pork so it opens like a book and lies flat. Rub the oil mixture over the inside of the pork shoulder. Season with salt and pepper. Roll the pork tightly and tie with butcher's twine.

In a large roasting pan, combine vegetables and wine. Add thyme and bay leaves. Place the pork on top of the vegetables. Rub the top of the pork with remaining olive oil and put the pan in the oven. Roast for 40 minutes, or until the skin is crispy. Brush the skin with pan juices and add a little of the chicken broth around the pork. Roast for another 3 hours, or until the internal temperature is at least 145°F, occasionally basting the skin with more chicken broth, keeping the pan moist.

Remove the pan from the oven and place the pork on a cutting board, discarding the twine. Let rest for 15 minutes. Arrange the vegetables on a serving platter and slice the pork. Pour pan juices over the pork and serve.

WITH HALIBUT, YOU NEED TO BE AN ARTIST. IT'S LIKE HAVING AN EMPTY CANVAS. YOU CREATE ANYTHING YOU WANT. WITH THAT SAID, YOU DON'T WANT TO OVERCOMPLICATE THE FISH; KEEP IT PURE.

IPPOGLOSSO AL VAPORE
STEAMED HALIBUT
SERVES 6

INGREDIENTS

1/4 CUP EXTRA-VIRGIN OLIVE OIL
4 CLOVES GARLIC, CHOPPED
1 MEDIUM YELLOW ONION, SLICED
8 PLUM TOMATOES, HALVED
1/2 CUP PITTED KALAMATA OLIVES, DICED
1 BUNCH ITALIAN PARSLEY, CHOPPED
1 TEASPOON CRUSHED RED PEPPER FLAKES
1 CINNAMON STICK
1 1/2 POUNDS HALIBUT
SALT AND PEPPER

INSTRUCTIONS

In a medium saucepan, heat olive oil over medium-low heat until shimmering. Cook garlic until soft but not browned. Add onion and cook until translucent. Increase the heat to medium-high and add tomatoes, cut side down. Cook the tomatoes, turning often, until they are soft. Stir in olives, parsley, red pepper flakes, salt, pepper and cinnamon stick. Cover and simmer on low heat for 15 minutes. Remove the cinnamon stick and purée the sauce in a food processor.

In a large saucepan, heat the sauce over medium heat. Cut halibut into 6 pieces. Add the halibut to the pan and cook, turning often, for about 8 minutes, or until the fish is cooked through. Remove from the heat. Serve the halibut with the sauce.

IN AMERICA, BRANZINO IS THE EQUIVALENT OF SEA BASS. THIS IS A SIMPLE BAKE USING FOIL, SLICED LEMONS AND OTHER FLAVORS. PUT IN THE OVEN AND DON'T FUSS. THE ONLY TOOL NEEDED IS A FORK. PUT THROUGH FOIL 25 MINUTES LATER, YOU KNOW FISH IS READY. IF YOU DOUBTING YOURSELF, YOU KNOW FISH IS READY.

BRANZINO
ROASTED BRANZINO WITH LEMONS
SERVES 4

INGREDIENTS

1 TABLESPOON EXTRA-VIRGIN
   OLIVE OIL
8 OUNCES PANCETTA, DICED
2 WHOLE BRANZINO, CLEANED
2 LEMONS, ZESTED
1/4 CUP CHOPPED FENNEL FRONDS
2 TABLESPOONS CHOPPED FRESH
   OREGANO
2 LEMONS, SLICED
1 MEDIUM WHITE ONION, SLICED
1/2 CUP CHARDONNAY
2 TABLESPOONS CHOPPED FRESH
   PARSLEY
SALT AND PEPPER

INSTRUCTIONS

Preheat oven to 400°F.

In a medium skillet, heat olive oil over medium heat until shimmering. Add pancetta and cook until the fat is rendered, about 8 minutes. Drain on a paper towel and set aside.

Line a baking sheet with aluminum foil. Rub the foil with olive oil. Lay fish on the foil and season with salt and pepper.

In a small bowl, combine lemon zest, fennel fronds and oregano. Spoon over the fish. Arrange lemon and onion slices on top of the fish. Sprinkle with pancetta and pour wine on top. Lay another piece of foil on top and crimp the edges to form a packet.

Roast until the fish is flaky, about 25 minutes. Remove from the baking sheet and let rest for 5 minutes. Remove the top piece of foil and arrange lemon slices and onions on a platter. Transfer the fish to the platter and garnish with parsley. Serve.

THIS IS MAURO

TAGLIATA CON RUCOLA
SIRLOIN WITH ARUGULA
SERVES 4

INGREDIENTS

3 CLOVES GARLIC, PEELED, SMASHED

1 TABLESPOON WHOLE BLACK PEPPERCORNS, CRUSHED

3 TABLESPOONS CHOPPED FRESH ROSEMARY

1 LARGE WHITE ONION, QUARTERED

1 TABLESPOON RED WINE VINEGAR

1/3 CUP EXTRA-VIRGIN OLIVE OIL

1 1/2 POUNDS SIRLOIN

6 CUPS ARUGULA

AGED BALSAMIC VINEGAR

2 BLOOD ORANGES

PARMIGIANO-REGGIANO SHAVINGS

SALT AND PEPPER

INSTRUCTIONS

In a medium bowl, combine garlic, peppercorns, rosemary, onion, red wine vinegar and olive oil. Add steak, making sure it is well coated with the marinade, and cover with plastic wrap. Refrigerate for 12 hours.

Bring the steak to room temperature. Season with salt and pepper. Preheat grill or heavy skillet over medium heat.

Cook the steak until desired doneness, about 4 minutes on each side for medium-rare. Remove the steak and let rest for 5 minutes.

Carve the steak diagonally into 1-inch strips across the grain. Arrange arugula on a serving platter and place the steak on top. Drizzle with balsamic vinegar and squeeze oranges over the top. Garnish with Parmigiano-Reggiano and pepper. Serve.

GUANCIALE DI MANZO
BAROLO BRAISED BEEF CHEEKS
SERVES 4

INGREDIENTS

2 1/2 POUNDS BEEF CHEEKS, CLEANED

2 CUPS BAROLO

1 1/4 CUPS CHOPPED WHITE ONION

3/4 CUP CHOPPED CELERY

1 TABLESPOON MINCED GARLIC

2 BAY LEAVES

2 SPRIGS FRESH ROSEMARY

1/2 TEASPOON WHOLE BLACK PEPPERCORNS

1/4 CUP EXTRA-VIRGIN OLIVE OIL

1 1/4 CUPS CHOPPED CARROTS

1/2 TABLESPOON TOMATO PASTE

2 CUPS CHICKEN BROTH (PAGE 69)

1 TEASPOON DRIED ITALIAN HERBS

1/4 TEASPOON CRUSHED RED PEPPER FLAKES

1 SPRIG THYME

1 SPRIG OREGANO

SALT AND PEPPER

INSTRUCTIONS

With a sharp knife, trim the extra fat and silverskin from the beef cheeks. Transfer the cheeks to a casserole dish and add 1 cup of Barolo, 1/4 cup onion, 1/2 cup celery, 1/2 tablespoon garlic, bay leaves, 1 sprig rosemary and the black peppercorns. Blend the ingredients and make sure the meat is covered by wine. Cover the dish with plastic wrap and refrigerate for 8 hours.

Preheat oven to 275°F.

In a large Dutch oven, heat half the olive oil over high heat until almost smoking. Remove the meat from the marinade and pat dry. Season both sides with salt and pepper. Add the meat to the oil and brown on all sides. Remove from the pan and set aside. Add the remaining oil, onion, celery, rosemary and carrots. Cook over medium-low heat for 20 minutes, or until the vegetables are soft. Add the remaining garlic and cook for 2 minutes. Add tomato paste and cook for 2 minutes. Strain the marinade and add to the pan. Add 1 cup Barolo. Bring to a boil and reduce by half. Add broth, mixed herbs, red pepper flakes, thyme, oregano and the beef. Stir well.

Cover and place in the oven. Cook for 3 hours, or until the cheeks are tender. Serve.

BRASATO DI POLLO
TOMATO AND WINE BRAISED CHICKEN
SERVES 4

INGREDIENTS

2 TABLESPOONS EXTRA-VIRGIN
   OLIVE OIL
1 CHICKEN (3 POUNDS), CUT INTO
   4 PIECES
1 SMALL WHITE ONION, DICED
2 TABLESPOONS MINCED GARLIC
1 TEASPOON FRESH THYME
1 TEASPOON FRESH SAGE
1 CUP DRY WHITE WINE
6 CUPS CANNED SAN MARZANO
   TOMATOES, DICED
2 TABLESPOONS TOMATO PASTE
2 TABLESPOONS CHOPPED FRESH
   PARSLEY
SALT AND PEPPER

INSTRUCTIONS

In a large skillet, heat 1 tablespoon olive oil over medium heat until shimmering. Pat the chicken pieces dry and add 2 pieces to the pan. Cook for 6 minutes, or until browned on all sides. Remove the chicken from the pan and set aside. Add another tablespoon of olive oil to the pan and cook the remaining chicken and set aside.

Reheat the skillet and add onion. Cook over medium heat until translucent. Add garlic, thyme and sage. Add wine and simmer for 3 minutes, stirring up the browned bits on the bottom. Add tomatoes and tomato paste. Cook for 2 minutes, stirring constantly.

Return the chicken to the pan and season with salt and pepper. Reduce the heat to low and cover. Simmer until the chicken is tender, about 40 minutes. Transfer the chicken to a serving platter and set aside.

Skim off excess fat from the liquid in the skillet and turn up the heat to high. Reduce the sauce and add salt and pepper to taste. Pour the sauce over the chicken and garnish with parsley. Serve.

DOLCE

CANNOLI
PASTRY SHELLS WITH WHIPPED RICOTTA **132**

PANNA COTTA
VANILLA CUSTARD **133**

GELATO
ITALIAN ICE CREAM **135**

TORTA ALL'ARANCIA
ORANGE CAKE **137**

TIRAMISU
CHOCOLATE ESPRESSO CAKE **139**

CANNOLI
PASTRY SHELLS WITH WHIPPED RICOTTA
SERVES 6

INGREDIENTS

1 POUND RICOTTA

2 CUPS CONFECTIONERS' SUGAR

1 TABLESPOON VANILLA EXTRACT

1/2 CUP MINI CHOCOLATE CHIPS

24 CANNOLI SHELLS

INSTRUCTIONS

In a large bowl, mix ricotta and sugar until combined. Add vanilla extract and chocolate chips. Fold gently. Pipe into cannoli shells and serve immediately or refrigerate.

PANNA COTTA
VANILLA CUSTARD
SERVES 4

INGREDIENTS

3 1/4 CUPS CONFECTIONERS'
  SUGAR
2 CUPS HEAVY CREAM
1 CUP WHOLE MILK
6 TEASPOONS UNFLAVORED
  GELATIN
1 CUP SEASONAL BERRIES
1 1/2 TABLESPOONS GRANULATED
  SUGAR

INSTRUCTIONS

In a medium saucepan, combine confectioners' sugar, cream and milk over medium-high heat, stirring constantly. Remove from the heat as the mixture starts to bubble but not boil. Pour in gelatin, stirring constantly. Continue stirring for 5 minutes. Pour into a medium bowl and stir occasionally while the mixture cools.

Once the mixture has cooled, pour into 4 to 6 ramekins. Refrigerate for 8 hours or overnight.

In a small bowl, combine berries and granulated sugar. Let stand for 1 hour.

When ready to serve, fill a small skillet with enough water to reach halfway up the sides of the ramekins. Bring the water to a simmer over medium-low heat. Use a flat knife to loosen the custard from the sides of the ramekins. Place each ramekin in the skillet for 2 seconds and then invert onto an individual serving plate, shaking gently to remove the custards from the ramekin. Spoon berries over the custard and serve.

GELATO
ITALIAN ICE CREAM
SERVES 4

INGREDIENTS

3 CUPS HEAVY CREAM
1 1/2 CUPS WHOLE MILK
1 CUP SUGAR
6 LARGE EGG YOLKS
1 1/2 CUPS PISTACHIO NUTS,
  TOASTED

INSTRUCTIONS

In a saucepan, bring cream, milk and sugar to a simmer over medium-low heat. Remove from the heat and let sit overnight in the fridge.

Bring the mixture back to a simmer and add yolks one at a time, constantly stirring, making sure they don't scramble. Cook until thickened. Strain into a bowl set over an ice bath and fold in pistachios. Let cool completely. Scoop into an aluminum container and freeze.

TORTA ALL'ARANCIA
ORANGE CAKE
SERVES 4

INGREDIENTS

2 CUPS PLUS 2 TABLESPOONS
   ALL-PURPOSE FLOUR

4 TABLESPOONS UNSALTED
   BUTTER, ROOM TEMPERATURE

1 CUP PLUS 3 TABLESPOONS SUGAR

3 LARGE EGGS

2 TABLESPOONS SAMBUCA

1 TABLESPOON WHOLE MILK

3 ORANGES, ZESTED

2 1/4 TEASPOONS BAKING POWDER

2 CUPS ORANGE JUICE

INSTRUCTIONS

Preheat oven to 350°F. Spray a 10-inch Bundt pan with cooking spray and dust with 2 tablespoons flour.

Using a mixer, combine butter and 1 cup sugar. Add eggs one at a time and mix after each addition. Add sambuca, milk and orange zest, mixing until combined. Slowly add remaining flour and mix until fully incorporated. Add baking powder and mix again.

Pour the mixture into the baking pan and bake for 45 minutes, or until the top of the cake is golden. Place the pan over a wine bottle to let cool.

Loosen the edges of the cake with a knife and invert onto a plate. With the end of a wooden spoon, poke holes into the cake.

In a small bowl, combine orange juice and remaining sugar. Pour the juice mixture into the holes and let the cake sit for about 1 hour to absorb the liquid.. Serve at room temperature.

TIRAMISU
CHOCOLATE ESPRESSO CAKE
SERVES 8

INGREDIENTS

1 QUART HEAVY CREAM

4 OUNCES CREAM CHEESE

4 OUNCES MASCARPONE

1 1/2 CUPS SUGAR

4 LARGE EGGS

3 CUPS BREWED COFFEE

1/2 CUP SWEET MARSALA

1 CUP BREWED ESPRESSO

1 PACKAGE (14 OUNCES)
   LADYFINGERS

COCOA POWDER

INSTRUCTIONS

In a large bowl, combine heavy cream, cream cheese, mascarpone, 1 cup sugar and eggs. Beat until well blended. Set aside.

In another large bowl, combine coffee, Marsala, espresso and remaining sugar. Dip each ladyfinger individually in the coffee mixture, soaking for a few seconds. Place in a single layer in a 9-by-11-inch glass pan with 3-inch sides. Add a 2-inch layer of the cream mixture. Add another layer of soaked ladyfingers and cream mixture. Smooth the surface and sprinkle with cocoa powder.

Cover with plastic wrap and refrigerate for 24 hours before serving.

INDEX